There is rich gleaning here for a[ ]
the authentic love of God in Chr[ ]
She clearly communicates the esteem Jesus has for all women with
scriptural references to the value of widows. This book is very relat-
able, with personal applications that help lead to good choices and
decisions. Widowhood: A Call to Leadership steers the reader away
from potential pitfalls into a victorious life anew. Best of all, Mary
highlights that widowhood, as well as other life changes, actually
becomes a calling of divine purpose that comes solely through the
invitation of God! Don't miss his invitation to lead.

—Lisa Crump
Vice-President, Volunteer Mobilization
Liaison to Prayer Ministries
National Day of Prayer Task Force

widowhood

a calling to leadership

widowhood

a calling to leadership

A CHANGED
PERSPECTIVE
ON LOSS

—

REDEMPTION
PRESS

mary bruce

Published by Redemption Press, PO Box 427, Enumclaw, WA 98022.

Toll-Free (844) 2REDEEM (273-3336)

Redemption Press is honored to present this title in partnership with the author. The views expressed or implied in this work are those of the author. Redemption Press provides our imprint seal representing design excellence, creative content, and high-quality production.

ISBN: 978-1-64645-052-7 (Paperback)
978-1-64645-053-4 (ePub)
978-1-64645-054-1 (Mobi)

Library of Congress Catalog Card Number: 2020906299

This book is dedicated to the memory of my mother,
who became a widow before I did
and who provided experience-based wisdom and compassion;
to my children, who loved me through all the ups and downs;
and to the Lord, who made Himself real in my time of need.

*He always comes alongside us to comfort us in every suffering so that
we can come alongside those who are in any painful trial. We can
bring them this same comfort that God has poured out upon us.*
2 Corinthians 1:4 TPT

contents

Preface   xi

Introduction   xiii

Chapter 1: What's in a Name?   17

Chapter 2: Living in Front of the Black Hole   21

Chapter 3: Invitation to the Journey and the Supplies Needed   27

Chapter 4: The Gift of Tears   33

Chapter 5: The List   39

Chapter 6: Do You See Yourself as Called or as a Volunteer?   43

Chapter 7: The Time of Aloneness   49

Chapter 8: A Study in Preparation—Both Elijah
and the Widow   57

Chapter 9: Loss of Expectation   63

Chapter 10: What's in a Name?—Baal or Ishi   69

Chapter 11: A New Bridal Veil   75

Chapter 12: Living in the Rest of My Life   81

Author's Note   85

Appendix A: Additional Resources   89

Appendix B: Ten Benefits of Being a Widow   91

preface

ALTHOUGH I AM A nurse by trade, I am not compassionate by nature. Rather than displaying compassion, I am more prone to looking for lessons in circumstances. My desire to see someone learn through a difficult circumstance can be a real turnoff when that person is hurting and needs comfort. I am a widow. True to my nature, I have tried to look for lessons in this role and to pass on my findings to others.

My initial idea of developing a widows' ministry was to see a network of widows helping one another. This did not happen.

I have been blessed in my attempts to develop friendships with widows. As widows, we all learn at our own pace and in God's timing, but I am confident that God has mighty plans for all of us while we are here. Through my own journey, God prepared my heart to shepherd and equip widows—whom I consider to each be leaders—to recognize their leadership potentials. Through this book, it is my hope that others can benefit from some of my life experiences: the good, the bad, and the ugly.

My picture of a ministry for widows is one that would provide a space for contemplation and reflection and a reset of vision and destiny. A widows' ministry should enable women to grow in their leadership skills and provide a place for fellowship where they can see themselves as precious, prepared, protected, and needed by God on this earth for kingdom purposes. I want widows to see themselves as leaders in their own spheres rather than as victims. It is my hope that my readers will recognize that better is a neighbor nearby than a brother far off, will glean a sense of fellowship with me as a fellow widow, and will develop a resolute partnership with God. I have learned much through the biographies of missionaries and fellow believers, and am prayerful that this book will provide hope for widows and those who want to help widows.

introduction

All widows begin second lives.
—Dorothy Gilman, *The Amazing Mrs. Polifax*

TWO SEEMINGLY UNRELATED TRAGEDIES became intimately intertwined in my life story, laying the foundation for my spiritual calling: to come alongside widows and help equip them to reach their leadership potentials. The beginnings of this calling were sadly initiated with the death of my dear husband, Ron, on a dark Friday early in September 2001. As I sat on the back-porch stoop the morning after his death, I looked to the heavens and said, *Here I am; it's you and me, God.* I had no idea then what God had in store or how I would use my loss to help others. Mere days later, thousands of people lost their lives in the 9/11 attacks on our country. Perhaps the initiation of my spiritual calling began on that September 11 morning as my twenty-two-year-old daughter and I bagged up my husband's clothing, while unspeakable terrors were unfolding just a hundred miles from my home. Or maybe the beginnings of my calling came a week later when we buried my husband's ashes and I realized that hundreds of other widows were also arranging funerals, while some were still looking for their loved one's bodies in the rubble.

If you've opened this book, you are either a widow looking for help in navigating your new life as a single woman, or you're a church-ministry leader interested in a new perspective.

For you who are widows, this is a Christian perspective on aloneness, dependence on God, and the leadership that can ensue. As a widow, you can begin to identify with church leaders who often experience a taste of aloneness in their leadership positions— that sense of being the only one totally responsible for important decision-making that affects others. One definition of loneliness has marked my widowhood and is displayed on a wall plaque from the Gotthard Institute: "Loneliness is my opportunity to identify with the Father in heaven when he sent Jesus out of heaven to earth." I am grateful that the Father understands my emotions in loss and that it forces me to be reliant upon him. For you who are church leaders, can you see the potential in sharing how your aloneness in leadership has brought about dependency upon God? I urge you to be mindful of encouraging widows by sharing your testimonies of dependence.

I know firsthand the many traumatic effects of widowhood. It severs emotional ties that may need to be acknowledged, identified, and confronted. There are many books to help widows and widowers through such struggles and through coping with aloneness. A list of some of my book recommendations can be found in Appendix A. But I hope this book will give you hope for your future as you recognize how the energy from the stress of your loss can be put into good, productive use for godly leadership.

Each widow is beautifully unique, sharing in God's calling of leadership. We immediately became leaders and heads of our families and households upon the deaths of our husbands. If you are a parent, as I am, you became the sole parent of your children. You may have become the owner of two or three cars, the go-to person for more than one house, the decision-maker for the camper or retirement home, the landlord for the condo or time-share, the fix-it person for broken pipes, the holder of keys without knowing which works where, and the instant memory-keeper for the family. One widow I know inherited her husband's company with 273 employees! These are reasons why I see widows as leaders within our own spheres of influence, and I hope you, too, grow to see yourself as competent, powerful, and influential.

For you who are church leaders, I hope that this book will stir you to see widows in a new way: as leaders needing direction and mentoring, as dynamic and overlooked potential within your congregations, and as untapped resources in the American church today. Look for her previous successes and help her see them through objective eyes. Engage her in her past interests and help her identify what to keep or leave in the past. It is my hope that this book will challenge every church leader and open a new way of thinking, to view widows as leaders rather than as burdens, victims, or projects needing attention.

chapter one

WHAT'S IN A NAME?

The name we give to something shapes our attitude to it.
—Katherine Patterson

*WIDOW, noun [Latin] A woman who has lost
her husband by death.*
—Webster's 1828 Dictionary

WHAT'S IN A NAME? If we live long enough, we will find an accumulation of names we call ourselves, often based on roles or names we've been given by others. We may call ourselves nurse, doctor, pastor, teacher, mother, or sister—all roles that may define us. In today's world, we Google name meanings months before our unborn babies make their entrance, looking for names that will perfectly describe the image and characteristics we hope for our little ones. In the past, names were passed down from generation to generation, often based on the positive attributes of the namesake. For example, I am my grandmother's namesake. The word *Mary* comes from the Greek root word "bitter root," which I hope doesn't define my grandmother or me!

I much prefer a different description of myself that was given to me quite innocently by a child but made a huge impact in my life. As I worked in a classroom at Sunday school, the pastor's son instructed another child: "Go give these to Mrs. Bruce." The other child responded, "Who's that?" The pastor's son answered, "The one who loves children." From that day forward, I've thought of myself as *the one who loves children*, a name worthy of effort. I have other names as well: nurse; wife of thirty-four years; "Miss Mercy," another name given to me by a young child; "Piedad," given by a peer at work; mother of two; homeschooling pioneer; grandmother of four—Mimi for my daughter's children and Marmie for my son's children; prayer warrior; intercessor; National Day of Prayer ministry leader; child of God; and widow.

As a woman, you may have many names and many titles, but widow is not one you planned for. Widow is a word used only to denote life in the past, not in the future. Before widowhood, you may have handled money matters, arranged family schedules, managed the shopping, and run the home. All of these responsibilities can make the transition to widowhood easier, though you may not have previously identified them as strong leadership points. Widowhood automatically places you as head of household, head of your husband's business, head of the family, and sole parent. What you call yourself and how you recognize your strong characteristics will move you forward through the season of loss into your new leadership role.

As you begin to envision your future without your mate, you may fall back on habits, traits, and expressions of your own personality before marriage. Marriage brings necessary accomodations. Once those thoughtful accomodations for the benefit of another are no longer necessary, you may slip into habits of youth, such as "burning the candle at both ends" or letting the housekeeping or bill paying go until stress forces action. Now you bring wisdom from life lessons and maturity from experiences gleaned through your married days to your new position as widow. Trust in your abilities and lean on God as you make the many decisions you will be forced to make. Remember your strong characteristics as you make decisions, such as which car to keep and who is going to help you with tasks your spouse covered. (I recommend waiting a year to make major decisions, but I recognize that isn't always practical.) Welcome the everyday realities—such as feeding the dog, tending the garden, going back to work, and cooking dinner—as tasks that will help you adapt to your new normal. Keeping your focus on God will also play a vital role in walking through your grief.

Early in my nursing career, I learned about the fight or flight responses that the human body triggers in reaction to perceived threats or real stress. In my own life, I recognized that my reaction to stress is the flight response, so I learned to harness my flight tendency by looking at my calendar and setting goals. This practice has been a relief for my mental health, giving me control on whether to work on something or not!

After Ron died, however, I recognized a third option to flight or fight. Each morning for that first year, I would sit on the back stoop before sunrise and listen for God, waiting for a sense of his presence to overcome me, and then appreciate the individuality of each pre-dawn sky and sunrise. During winter months, wrapped in my coat, boots, and blanket, I would enjoy the stillness before the start of a new day. This became a place of solitude and a space of refuge, where I took comfort in being a child of God and embraced Psalm 46:10: "Be still and know that I am God!"

Dear sister, is your focus on the past or is your focus on the future? If you are not a morning person, can you identify a time in your day that is completely free of interruption where you can wait for a sense of God's presence to overcome you? Reading through the Psalms on a regular basis can help move your focus onto the character of God and direct your thoughts to him. Try reading five psalms a day: one recommendation is to start with the "Psalm of the day"—for example on the third day of the month, read Psalm 3, and then read Psalm 33, Psalm 63, Psalm 93, and Psalm 123, adding the number thirty each time. On the fourth day of the month, read Psalms 4, 34, 64, 94, and 124. In this way you will read through the complete book within a month; we save Psalm 119 for day 31, since it is a long psalm. Try this for one year. Be sure to jot down your thoughts, prayers, and questions in a journal. You will be blessed by God.

Church leader, do you recognize your own fight or flight response to stressful situations? How do you process the many stressors that encroach upon your oneness with God and your peace? Do you see each unexpected call as an interruption or as an opportunity to practice the character of Christ? How do you protect your personal devotion time and keep it as a time of the day when you can restore yourself and find yourself in the God of Israel, our fortress, as David did? Read through Psalm 46 and picture yourself in ancient Israel.

chapter two

LIVING IN FRONT
OF THE BLACK HOLE

I thought I could describe a state; make a map of sorrow.
Sorrow, however,
turns out to be not a state but a process.
—C. S. Lewis, *A Grief Observed*

THERE IS NO WAY to begin any sharing on the calling of widowhood without having experienced this phenomenon and without acknowledging that we are all in different places with loss. This is true for all who suffer loss, regardless of age, gender, ethnicity, race, or geographical location. Loss, whether expected or unexpected, touches on every other unresolved loss within.

> GRIEF, noun [Latin gravis]. The pain of mind produced
> by loss, misfortune, injury or evils of any kind; sorrow;
> regret. We experience grief when we lose a friend, when
> we incur loss, when we consider ourselves injured, and
> by sympathy, we feel grief at the misfortunes of others.
> *(Webster's 1828 Dictionary)*

Before Ron died, I had more experience with death than the average person. I had been a nurse for more than thirty years, worked with hospice patients, and been present at the passing of several family members. But when it was my turn to experience loss of a spouse, I didn't know how to grieve. I had a visible picture of grief as a black hole dragging along behind me, like a moveable manhole without the cover, just waiting for me to be caught off guard and to step backward and fall in. And despite being a believer for thirty-five years, I envisioned that I would be overcome in the dark hole by some evil, unknown force. I actually spent months in this thought condition. My black hole was how I pictured grief, and I wanted none of it. Then, while sitting at Singing Beach in Manchester-by-the-Sea, Massachusetts, I pictured that black hole like a large, upside-down, paper bag ready to invert itself over my head and swallow me up. The black hole had a life of its own. I can now laugh when I look back at that image, but somehow this image had become my definition of grief.

Fortunately God broke into my thinking that morning on the beach and reminded me that even if I fell in a pit or was swallowed up by darkness, Jesus would be with me there too. David, too, took comfort in knowing that God was with him in his darkness: "If I say, 'Surely the darkness will overwhelm me, and the light around me will be night, even the darkness is not dark to You, and the night is as bright as the day. Darkness and light are alike to You'" (Psalm 139:11–12 NASB). From that point on, fear no longer had a grip on me, but I still tended to avoid grief at all costs. In their book *How People Grow*, Henry Cloud and John Townsend say, "Grief is the one pain that heals all others. Grief is the most important pain there is." C. H. Spurgeon considers liquid petitions (tears) as being distilled from the heart: "to distill," means to "separate and change from one substance to another." This word beautifully describes God's renewing work in the midst of our tears.

For years I did as David did: I hid in the praises. I immersed myself in worship, became a worshipaholic, and loved being loved by the Lord in those joyful moments. Others reflected that I was over my loss because I looked so happy in the Lord, but in fact, I was really hiding. Each of us has a unique path to walk through our time of loss.

You may have heard of Elizabeth Kubler-Ross, a Swiss psychiatrist who published a study in 1969 about death and dying. I relied upon her principles in my nursing career and knew her work inside and out. She characterized the emotions of the dying process as denial, anger, bargaining, depression, and acceptance. She made these observations while working with cancer victims.

Truthfully, we often go through these emotions with any great loss: loss of a spouse, a child, a job, our expectations, a home. Any loss—even small ones, either expected or unexpected—can trigger emotions of grief, and they don't come in neat order. We can be angry one day and in denial the next, or we can be in bargaining mode and then angry. Losing something less significant, like a pet or even a set of keys, can be the straw that breaks the camel's back or the trigger to the denied flood of emotions. Not everyone sails through the stages of loss in neat order. I watched this happen with my husband years before his illness. We were living in Florida when his grandmother died in Connecticut. He had been close to her and was very saddened but would not go north to grieve with the family or attend the funeral. Our dog died about a year later, close to the anniversary of his grandmother's death. Ron broke down and wept uncontrollably. The less significant death of our dog triggered the emotional flood he had been storing over his grandmother's passing since he had not been there with family.

For widows these phases come at different times of realization of our loss and may be repeated as we grow through this difficult period. My husband's memorial service was on Monday, September 10, with 9/11 occurring the next morning on Tuesday. There was a call from ministry leadership on Wednesday to host prayer at every state capitol that Friday. I wrestled with my ability to lead this within our state but ultimately fulfilled the request. It was denial of my personal loss. *Just keep going, pretend it doesn't hurt, keep on smiling, and push through the pain.*

Although I tried several grief groups, I did not connect well and was unsure whom to trust with my feelings. I had a very small business, teaching scrapbooking and selling supplies. I remember being angry with students one day, trying to convince them of the importance of preserving memories. *Couldn't they see the importance, the value? Look at me—I don't have that person with whom to make new memories or even discuss old memories.* I quit the business that day. My anger was not really with them but with my loss. Friends, who saw my activities as causing me to be too busy, commended me for putting the business aside, but years later I regretted quitting.

My social relationships also changed during that early transition to widowhood. Couples we had been friends with and spent dinners with didn't fit the same way when one man was missing. My evenings together with others shifted. This inadvertent isolation is something that happens, that hurts, and that changes social structure for any widow. Depression was easy to embrace.

We were under contract for reconstruction of our kitchen when my husband died, and I went ahead with the plan. That in itself was denial! As with many reconstruction projects, the project entailed more than expected, and the house was opened to the cold weather for a short period of time. I took to sleeping in our sleeping bag as a comfort not just from the cold, but as a reminder of Ron. I ate tuna straight from the can, one of his absolute favorites, but something that had been revolting to me; I didn't even like tuna salad. It was as if I needed to prolong the relationship through comforts of his.

Because the house was under construction and non-construction days held painful memories, my favorite place became worship rehearsals at church. Although I wasn't playing regularly with the Sunday worship team, I was rehearsing regularly with the team and taking comfort from music at home. I needed as many reminders of God's love as I could find. Worship became my place of joy.

Although my days were filled with activities, my alone times were often consumed with reminders of my husband.

> The deeper that sorrow carves into your being, the more joy you can contain. Is not the cup that holds your wine the very cup that was burned in the potter's oven? (Kahlil Gibran, 1883–1931)

chapter three

INVITATION TO THE JOURNEY
AND THE SUPPLIES NEEDED

*And this same God who takes care of me will supply all
your needs from his glorious riches, which have been given
to us in Christ Jesus.*
Philippians 4:19

No TEACHING ABOUT WIDOWHOOD can start without a
widow, and as Aslan, a God-representative in C. S. Lewis's
book *The Chronicles of Narnia*, would say, "This is Mary's story."
The year: 2001.

The invitation to widowhood came rather suddenly and at a
time when both my husband and I had been called into higher
levels of responsibility within two national ministries. Ron was an
active officer at the state level with the Gideons International, and
I was an active state leader with the National Day of Prayer Task
Force. We each were moving into more regional projects for our
ministries. We had just celebrated our thirty-fourth wedding anniversary.

My husband and I were pacing partners, reminding each other

of ministry needs, collaborating on tasks, and generally helping each other out. With our adult children both living out of the home, we enjoyed a routine centered around our work, ministries, and management of our five-acre farmland. We prayed together daily, attended and served in a local church, and knew about spiritual warfare. When Ron's illness required hospitalization, I stayed by his bedside as much as possible. On one occasion, I was scheduled to travel for two days. My plan was to cancel the travel and stay with him, but his direction to me was to go; he had his path, and I had mine. If we were both to flounder through the difficulty, there would be two of us off the spiritual battlefield. His military mindset propelled me through those days of a coming reality.

Ron's illness started with the swelling of his left elbow. He had been on a medication for cholesterol, and all of his regular blood work was negative for any issues. Since he had been mowing under some pines where he got caught in a web, the swelling was thought to be a spider bite. The swelling initially went down after he started antibiotics but then appeared on his other arm and on one of his legs. A visit back to his doctor on the last day of June showed an irregular heartbeat, and he began heart medication. Two weeks later in mid-July, his right leg was swollen. An ultrasound of his leg revealed a blood clot, as we had suspected. The moment we heard the doctor's report about the extent of the clot was the moment we realized that this was not just a physical ailment but also a spiritual calling—a charge to hold fast to the faith we had already spoken of and a call to demonstrate godliness, faith, perseverance, and integrity unto the end. With our two different perspectives and one God and one belief system, this was an opportunity to affect the local body of Christ with encouragement and hope.

The ultrasound had revealed a long clot, the entire length of his leg, and he was admitted and started on intravenous blood thinners. After a shower the next day, Ron fell onto the bed writhing in pain. He was given medication and sent to ultrasound again, this time of his belly. The doctors suspected that a clot had broken off and was causing the pain. The abdominal CAT scan confirmed that he had a very aggressive cancer of the mucous membrane throughout his entire body and that clots were being thrown from his liver. Two attempts at chemotherapy were disastrous, and Ron and I embarked on our new normal as he began hospice at home with meds for pain control. Details of our daily life blurred as friends came and went during the remaining weeks of his life.

Ron seemed to be at peace. One day while I was standing beside his hospital bed, he told a visitor, "Whether I live or die, it really doesn't matter. I'll be with Jesus, and it will be the best." In that moment, looking down at my ailing husband, I thought, *Yes, but if you die, is that God's best for me?* We've all heard Romans 8:28: "And we know that God causes everything to work together for the good of those who love God and are called according to his purpose for them." Could that include the extremes such as death of a spouse? I knew immediately I had a choice: Do I take God at His Word, or do I deny God's intention for my best? This was my moment of invitation to widowhood. I chose to consciously accept God's grace in that moment—grace to believe that even if my husband died, it would be God's best for him and God's best for me. Did I really believe that God could use loss, abandonment, and pain for my best? Truthfully, I didn't think of these things. They were in the blurry cloud of uncertainty and change surrounding sickness. My mind agreed with the Word of God, but my heart took a little longer—several years, actually.

Many visitors found it hard to believe that Ron was near death, as he continued communication with the ministry and his workplace. The last week of his life he insisted I drive him, with his walker and oxygen tank, to a ministry assignment about thirty miles from home, where he met with others and made calls to pastors. I left him with his partners but was astounded and angered to find him a few hours later by himself, as the others had left to fulfill appointments. When we returned again the next day, I sat with him until his portion of the assignment was completed. I was experiencing some of Kubler-Ross's anger. On the way home, we stopped at his workplace, where he told shocked colleagues that cancer was going to take his life and exhorted them that each of us needs to be ready to face God. He said goodbye to his team members, most of whom had no idea that he had been battling cancer. "This was the hardest thing I ever had to do," Ron said as we pulled out of the driveway. This was the only time I ever saw him cry.

As I reflect on his time of goodbyes, I remember the many people he led to Christ and his heart for those who were hungry for a relationship with God but who didn't acknowledge Jesus. It was hard for him to leave the ones he might not ever see again. We were both strong in the belief that we will see Jesus after death, so there was no real "goodbye" for us. But Ron grieved for those who did not acknowledge Jesus. After saying goodbye to his fellow workers, we listened to a recording of a song we'd never heard, "If You Could See Me Now." The lyrics speak about how pleasant heaven is compared to the reality, pain, and suffering of earth. That helped point the way of acceptance for both of us.

The next day, Ron called a friend he'd had since high school. I had not seen this friend in several years and was surprised to see him teeter down the driveway with his walker and announce that he was taking Ron out for the afternoon. Despite my objections, the two of them left with their walkers. What a sight to see these two buddies wobbling out to the car. They returned hours later, and his friend warned me: "Don't give him any pain meds for a few hours; he doesn't need them." When I asked why, he said they had spent the afternoon reminiscing in the wine cellar. Ron didn't ask for anything for pain until about ten o'clock that night. He slept through the night and the next morning went home to be with the Lord.

How we move through difficulty, anger, denial, bargaining, and acceptance is not always out loud or orderly. My husband, who often claimed that we need not speak every thought, was known as a man who only said what needed to be said. He moved through his last weeks with the same stoicism and determination he carried throughout our years of marriage. I saw him live out Philippians 3:14: "I press on to reach the end of the race and receive the heavenly prize for which God, through Christ Jesus, is calling us." As a nurse, I had seen many other patients and family members unto death, but I began my widowhood with the example of living life to its fullest for Jesus. The supplies we receive from God are not always visible. Ron's determination, perseverance, years of hard work, care for the lost, spiritual and emotional growth through several job changes, and military mindset were examples that prepared me for my future.

chapter four

THE GIFT OF TEARS

Those who plant in tears will harvest with shouts of joy.
They weep as they go to plant their seed, but they sing as
they return with the harvest.
Psalm 126:5–6

YEARS EARLIER, IN 1995, I had the opportunity to attend New Life Church in Colorado Springs, Colorado, a megachurch that sat about five thousand at each service. Prior to this, our fourteen-year-old son had spoken to us many times about the gift of speaking in tongues. He attended a school where one teacher prayed in this manner and our son frequently appealed to us to ask for this gift of the Holy Spirit for ourselves. This was a controversial manifestation, meaning that it often provoked ungodly controversy amongst ministries. Our solution had been to ignore the gift and continue serving. As I stood singing worship songs that Sunday morning in a front row of that expansive church, I almost mockingly said to the Lord: *All right, God. I'll take the gift of speaking in tongues.* My immature disrespect was evident even to me. Immediately, I began weeping, messy weeping, loud and sobbing weeping, which was hard to experience with a new teammate standing by and no tissues! I heard the Lord say: *I'm not giving you the gift of tongues; I'm giving you the gift of tears.*

When I shared this event with my husband later that night, he politely reminded me that the gift of tears wasn't listed as one of the biblical gifts. The next morning, I got the same answer from my son. But during the next year, God began a work in all three of us. When disappointments, thoughtless words, or hurtful incidents occurred, I began to experience sorrow instead of anger. As my husband and son began to recognize my different reactions and different perspectives on daily life, they became more sensitive, questioning, and considerate. I had received the gift of tears. I didn't understand it, but I got it. Like many of my generation, I had been told, "Buck up," "No crying," "You're the oldest," or "Set a good example," during my childhood. You may have been raised under the same parental guidance. It denies the value of truthful expressions of hurt and imposes the practice of stuffing emotion until it becomes destructive, either outwardly or inwardly. What was meant to teach maturity instead became destructive in many ways. Could there really be a gift of tears?

Here are some interesting facts about tears. Medical science identifies differences in tears for various reactions: laughing hysterically; wincing from acute and unexpected pain; or sorrow, suffering, and mourning. In researching through my nursing dictionary, I discovered that different chemicals are released dependent upon the cause of the tears, meaning the chemical composition of tears differs. Think about the wonder of the human body. "Tears brought about by emotions have a different chemical makeup than those for lubrication."[1] Additionally, if you are in a fight or flight physical response, your brain automatically turns off the lacrimal glands that produce tears to prevent them from interfering with eyesight needed to fight or flee. Hmmm....

God's Word, written thousands of years earlier, also describes

---

[1] *Mosby's Medical Dictionary*, 8th edition (Elsevier, 2009).

differences in tears. According to the *Spirit-Filled Life Bible Commentary*, there are six different types listed in Scripture.[2]

1. Tears of sorrow: 2 Kings 20:5. "Go back to Hezekiah, the leader of my people. Tell him, 'This is what the Lord, the God of your ancestor David, says, I have heard your prayer and seen your tears. I will heal you, and three days from now you will get out of bed and go to the Temple of the Lord.'"

2. Tears of joy: Genesis 33:4. "Then Esau ran to meet him and embraced him, threw his arms around his neck, and kissed him. And they both wept."

3. Tears of compassion: John 11:35. "Then Jesus wept."

4. Tears of desperation: Esther 4:1. "When Mordecai learned about all that had been done, he tore his clothes, put on burlap and ashes, and went out into the city, crying with a loud and bitter wail."

5. Tears of travail (giving birth): Isaiah 42:14. "He will say, 'I have long been silent; yes, I have restrained myself. But now, like a woman in labor, I will cry and groan and pant.'"

6. Tears of repentance: Joel 2:12–13. "That is why the Lord says, 'Turn to me now, while there is time. Give me your hearts. Come with fasting, weeping, and mourning. Don't tear your clothing in your grief, but tear your hearts instead.' Return to the Lord your God, for he is merciful and compassionate, slow to get angry and filled with unfailing love. He is eager to relent and not punish."

Regardless of your tear types, God will meet you. I remember losing a pregnancy late in the first trimester. A friend stopped by on her way to church after my husband had taken the children to

---

[2] *New Spirit-Filled Life Bible*, ed. Jack Hayford, "Advancing in Kingdom Dynamics," Psalm 126:5–6, "Tears and Brokenness in Victorious Warfare" (Thomas Nelson Inc., 2002, 2013), 730.

service. She brought me a refrigerator magnet with a picture of a barn, nearly identical to the one on our property, which read, "The Lord draws near to the broken hearted," from Psalm 34:18. I read that statement several times and, crying out in angry despair, I screamed into the emptiness of the house after she had left, "Is that true?" As I stood in the kitchen, feeling as empty as my house that morning, I was overwhelmed by a deep peace, and I sensed the Lord saying, *When you have nothing more to give, no energy for anything, I do the action; I draw near to you.* Friends, meeting with him in the truth and intimacy of your tears will be a most unusual and comforting experience. Knowing yourself, your weaknesses, and your vulnerabilities, while recognizing God's total provision in your brokenness, can be the strongest leadership qualities you bring into your future.

Church leaders, have you read the sermon "Jesus Wept," by Charles Spurgeon? He considers tears as liquid prayers. Think on these quotes:

1. "Let us learn to think of tears as liquid prayers; and of weeping as a constant dropping of importunate intercession which will wear its way right surely into the very heart of mercy, despite the stony difficulties which obstruct the way."[3]

2. "The tears of John, which were his liquid prayers, were so far as he was concerned, the sacred keys by which the sealed book was opened" (Rev. 5:4).[4]

3. "No prayer will ever prevail with God more surely than a liquid petition, which, being distilled from the heart, trickles from the eye, and waters the cheek."[5]

---

[3] Charles H. Spurgeon, *The Treasury of David: Psalms*, vol. 1, "Psalm 6," (Crossway, 1993).

[4] *Morning and Evening*, by Charles H. Spurgeon, revised by Alistair Begg (Crossway, 2003).

[5] Charles H. Spurgeon, *The Complete Works of C. H. Spurgeon*, vol. 35, #32091, section 3 (Delmarva Publications, 2012).

There is great value in the shedding of tears for ourselves, both physically and emotionally. Tears can wash the eyes, release chemicals, and help release pent-up emotions. Crying is the healthy reaction to pain and loss; stuffing the emotional response compresses the emotion into anger, which often explodes at the wrong time and for the wrong reasons. However, there is also great value in the shedding of our tears for others. As leaders, we can set an example of the correct response to pain and suffering. Are we set for that? Do we have a stash of tissues and empty trash bags ready for our tears? Leaders lead. Our tears can help some people open their own hearts, examine their own responses, and consider life from a different perspective. Shedding tears can show compassion and honesty and be a truthful reminder that we "are all parts of the same body," according to Ephesians 4:25.

Challenge: Read "Jesus Wept," by Charles Haddon Spurgeon.[6]

---

[6] Sermon No. 2,091, vol. 35, Scripture: John 11:35, Metropolitan Tabernacle Pulpit (June 23, 1889).

chapter five

THE LIST

Discretion will protect you,
and understanding will guard you.
Proverbs 2:11

The LORD is my rock, my fortress, and my savior; my God
is my rock, in whom I find protection. He is my shield,
the power that saves me, and my place of safety.
Psalm 18:2

S EVERAL MONTHS AFTER MY Ron's death, I represented the National Day of Prayer ministry at a large event in Boston. My display was large and bulky and difficult to set up, but I managed with help from other vendors. I was grateful that my son, who lived about thirty miles away, was coming to help me dismantle and pack up the display. He took the train in and helped me before we took the car back to his home to enjoy dinner with his fiancé. Over dinner, he raised the possibility that one of the men at the event had been "hitting" on me. I was quite surprised at his observation and wondered if he was being confronted with the possibility of new people entering his life in a new way. I remembered how one man who had attended my husband's funeral approached me at that time to offer himself to help take Ron's place. This man's insensitivity and timing was a turnoff and a warning to me. Mentally and emotionally I shut the door to any kind of male relationships, recognizing that there would be men who might want to replace my husband. No one can replace another person. So in response to my son's question, and still being a new widow, I wrote three things on my napkin and pushed it across the table. They were qualifications for a next life mate: someone who could lead me in worship and prayer, someone with comparable energy and drive for ministry, and someone financially free who would enjoy helping me with that aspect of my life. We all laughed at the difficulty in finding one person with all of these qualities.

I don't remember carrying that paper home with me, but I found it several years later in the bottom of a seldom-used dish, and I added a few more detailed qualifications to the list. I needed to protect myself from me, from emotional insecurity of widowhood, and from my own insecurities as a woman. I remember feeling safe from my own emotions and the errors of past emotional decisions, knowing that I would be protected if I held to my list of standards. The chances of finding all those specifics in one man were nearly impossible. I wouldn't succumb to a random encounter that could affect my future, whatever that was going to be, because whoever it was would have to meet the standards of the list.

Two years passed and, lo and behold, I found a member of our church who met the qualifications. I actually went directly home and checked the list. Sure enough, he met every one of my protective standards, with only one exception: he was thirty years younger than I! I don't know how long I laughed at that, but a message came to me from the Lord: *Mary, do you think that you can outdo me? If there is one man who fits at your church and he's too young, don't you think that I could have someone else your age?* I realized in that moment that not only had I been protecting myself from men, but I had also been protecting myself from even God. He may have brought others along the way whom I ignored because they didn't fit my list. Sitting on the floor in my bedroom, my laughter merged into tears of regret and repentance for thinking I could protect my-self without relying upon God.

I wish I could say that I rested in this knowledge that God could bring someone to me, but my old flesh rose up again one day when I was late for a prayer meeting and came in during introductions. There were several new people present in the small group, and one caught my attention. Truthfully, I only remembered the worship and prayer qualifications on my list, but as the meeting progressed, I wondered about this visitor and remained distracted during the prayer time. Afterward, I found myself thinking of ways to engage in conversation, but it never happened. Finally, the Lord impressed upon me that I was a well-known member of the group and that I would be easy to connect with through my ministry and friends. Others could easily find me, with no need for me to initiate.

As I walked away from that gathering, I felt a new sense of freedom, a deeper love for God, an urgency to continue on the path he has for me, and a true sense of protection. He will arrange the connections. He will be my protector not only from others but also from my own mistakes, wrong decisions, and my emotional self. Proverbs 15:25 (NASB) reminds us, "The LORD will tear down the house of the proud, but He will establish the boundary of the widow." He confirmed my purpose in his kingdom work and his protection over me in the accomplishments of it.

God has still not opened the door for a new husband. He has opened the door to several male friends who lead me in worship, help with financial freedom, and serve passionately in ministry, just not all in one man. Sometimes I wallow in aloneness, wishing I had a partner for things like dinners, movies, and walks—someone with the same interests who would do some of the initiating! But that is not the fulfillment of marriage vows. I have male friends whom I respect and love with agape love. Years ago, one male friend told me he was looking for a WIFE: Worshipper, Intercessor, Friend of

God and Friend for him, and Encourager. These are great qualifications for any relationship.

In your own loss, be mindful in determining if you are so focused on your loss, both consciously and unconsciously, that you do not see the positives of your life. Ask God to remind you of his works in your life. Read aloud 2 Samuel 22:26–35.

chapter six

DO YOU SEE YOURSELF AS CALLED OR AS A VOLUNTEER?

We even saw giants there, the descendants of Anak.
Next to them we felt like grasshoppers,
and that's what they thought, too!
Numbers 13:33

THROUGH THESE YEARS OF running with the Lord of Hosts, my Adventurer, I have come to realize that widowhood is a calling. It is not something we plan on when we get married. We don't think about it when everything is going well. We don't choose the timing of it. It is a calling from the Lord, not a volunteer opportunity in which we can decide to un-volunteer. Many widows may have never thought of their loss as any sort of opportunity or considered the perspective in which they could view their loss. The opposite of choosing to see loss as an opportunity is to see loss as a victim. Victim mentality may lead to an unhealthy method of communicating, especially in moments of crisis. How we approach life—the good, the bad, and the ugly—affects everything we think and do, almost in the same way wearing sunglasses colors everything we see.

Victim mentality is always ready to blame someone or something for one's own internal peace and overall well-being. If I can blame another when I'm unsettled, then I don't have to take responsibility for my own responses and choices. All of us will go through ups and downs in life, but how we view those ups or downs can be evidence of our own mindset.

I have worked on projects with many volunteers. Some volunteers with victim mentality come with preconceived ideas that are not easy to understand or work with, such as giving minimum effort, rejecting constructive criticism, complaining, being unprepared, and failing to recognize their own worth. Of course there are paid workers like this too, but all have the opportunity to grow. This is where church leaders can help the widow during crisis—not by doing the work, but by helping truth to be revealed in loving, accepting ways and continuing to build up the worth of that widow through growth.

Volunteering encompasses the freedom to un-volunteer. Widows cannot un-volunteer. Widows may have been individuals who gave minimum effort in the past, but now they are given the opportunity to change that. For all of the areas in which minimum effort was formerly extended, without their husbands around, widows will more than likely need to put out more effort. Even decision-making will require more emotional effort and strength than previously needed, especially when young children are involved. These are the opportunities God provides for widows to depend on him. Rather than complaining, widows will need to tackle problems head on, such as losing power in a storm, loss of heat on a cold night, dealing with a sick child, or experiencing car problems. All of these problems require immediate action, which inevitably leads to firsthand experience with leadership. The widow may see her inadequacies in dealing with issues but should be reminded of her growth in leadership.

Widowhood may cause some widows to feel trapped, caught in some undesirable, unwanted situation, imprisoned in bad luck, and overwhelmed with details that escalate with the stressful pain of loss. What were normal, daily life patterns become wishful thinking as the pain of grief magnifies problems. This is where God steps in to those who call on him. He calls back to them. This is where the church can help: affirming for them the beauty of widowhood and God's calling on their lives to a more intimate relationship with him. According to *Webster's 1828 Dictionary*, a calling is "a divine summons, a vocation, and invitation." When widows learn they have a calling, they will begin to see themselves as invited by God into a higher calling. God is not forcing himself but rather offering this invitation to a deeper intimacy. Sacrifices, struggles, pain, and issues can be met when we call on the Lord for help.

A friend who just recently became a widow exclaimed, "People are trying to comfort me with words like 'Oh, when my mama died . . .' or 'when my papa died . . .', but this is different!" Losing a spouse is different than any other loss because marriage involves the spiritual aspect of covenant before God, and he wants to meet you in the spiritual void that occurs with the loss of your partner. This is where he comes to invite you into deeper relationship with him to fill that spiritual void. Paul says it like this in 1 Corinthians 7:32, "I want you to be free from the concerns of this life. An unmarried man can spend his time doing the Lord's work and focusing on how to please him. But a married man has to think about his earthly responsibilities and how to please his wife. His interests are divided. In the same way, a woman who is no longer married or has never been married can be devoted to the Lord and holy in body and in spirit. But a married woman has to think about her earthly responsibilities and how to please her husband" (1 Cor. 7:32–34).

Widowhood is certainly not something to be envied, nor is it something to be frowned upon or looked down upon. It is a calling from the Lord and an invitation to greater intimacy with God. It is an occasion for self-examination, an introduction to further humility and dependence, and an opportunity for deeper prayer.

The church commissions missionaries, pastors, church workers, and ministry leaders, but we do not commission widows. Yet, this is where the church can help: by recognizing the great value God places on widows. He chooses to be the defender of widows (Ps. 68:5) and their provider (Deut. 16:11–14). God will punish those who harm widows.

Many ministries today clump widows and single women together, a perspective with which I disagree. Singles who may have been married and divorced, singles who were living together and decided to separate, singles by choice or life circumstances, or singles who have been abandoned by the father of their children are often treated with the same regard as widows. Each of these groups has some common challenges, but these situations all hold the possibility of the single person being confronted face to face with the former partner. That cannot happen with true widows. Death is permanent. Emotional widows and singles by circumstance have a different row to hoe, a painful and difficult path. Common challenges such as housing, finances, relationships, and child rearing may exist, but for the widow there are no potential interactions or issues with a spouse. There is no turning back from the death of a spouse. It is permanent.

Despite the fact that women were considered second-class citizens in biblical times and that widows were the lowest of the low, there are more than eighty verses in the Bible related to widows. Perhaps this is why God so values them: "Though the LORD is great, he cares for the humble, but he keeps his distance from the proud" (Ps. 138:6).

In biblical times, there was a system of practical steps in providing for widows: the brother of a widow's husband had responsibility to take in the widow, near kinsman had the opportunity to redeem her, and children and nephews had certain responsibilities. Widows of childbearing age had certain instructions and the "widow indeed" was to be cared for by the church. In my desire to be the best widow I could, I needed to know God's perspective on widowhood, so I looked up every verse in *Strong's Concordance* about widows. In reviewing those verses, I could see that there is a great purpose in being called into widowhood. It is a privilege and a direct invitation from God to grow in faith, as we choose to believe that he truly does want the best for each of us. I discovered the calling of widowhood in a frequently quoted story from Scripture, not so much by the widow but by the one whom God brought to the widow. The story is in 1 Kings 17:1–16.

chapter seven

THE TIME OF ALONENESS

Now she who is really a widow, and left alone,
trusts in God and continues in supplications and prayers
night and day.
1 Timothy 5:5 NKJV

A FTER MANY PROMPTINGS, I registered at our church for a Bible study on the motivational spiritual gifts found in Romans 12:6–8. Our homework assignment was to read 1 Kings 17–19. I couldn't get past the first several verses:

> Now Elijah the Tishbite, who was of the settlers of Gilead, said to Ahab, "As the LORD, the God of Israel lives, before whom I stand, surely there shall be neither dew nor rain these years, except by my word." The word of the LORD came to him, saying, "Go away from here and turn eastward, and hide yourself by the brook Cherith, which is east of the Jordan. It shall be that you will drink of the brook, and I have commanded the ravens to provide for you there." So he went and did according to the word of the LORD, for he went and lived by the

brook Cherith, which is east of the Jordan. The ravens brought him bread and meat in the morning and bread and meat in the evening, and he would drink from the brook. It happened after a while that the brook dried up, because there was no rain in the land. Then the word of the Lord came to him, saying, "Arise, go to Zarephath, which belongs to Sidon, and stay there; behold, I have commanded a widow there to provide for you." So he arose and went to Zarephath, and when he came to the gate of the city, behold, a widow was there gathering sticks; and he called to her and said, "Please get me a little water in a jar, that I may drink." As she was going to get it, he called to her and said, "Please bring me a piece of bread in your hand." But she said, "As the Lord your God lives, I have no bread, only a handful of flour in the bowl and a little oil in the jar; and behold, I am gathering a few sticks that I may go in and prepare it for me and my son, that we may eat it and die." Then Elijah said to her, "Do not fear; go, do as you have said, but make me a little bread cake from it first and bring it out to me, and afterward you may make one for yourself and for your son. For thus says the Lord God of Israel, 'The bowl of flour shall not be exhausted, nor shall the jar of oil be empty, until the day that the Lord sends rain on the face of the earth.'" So she went and did according to the word of Elijah, and she and he and her household ate for many days. The bowl of flour was not exhausted nor did the jar of oil become empty, according to the word of the Lord which He spoke through Elijah." (1 Kings 17:1–16 NASB)

Note, in the first verse Elijah says dew and rain would come only by his word. Who was this man of God that had the king's ear? This is the first biblical documentation of Elijah, a mighty prophet who eventually walked right out of this world with God in 2 Kings 2:1–15. We know how he left this earth, but where did he come from? How did he get to be so influential? Today he might be described as a very important person, a counselor to the head of state, someone who understood government principles and policies, or perhaps as an attorney or someone with a relationship to a president or king. We know from his ability to come before a king that there was some preparation to this point. As I read this passage, I wondered what preparation God has allowed in my life to bring me to this point?

Was it audacity, mere confidence, or a slip of the tongue for Elijah to say there wouldn't be rain until it fell by "*my* word" rather than by "*God's* word"? Aren't we always supposed to be directing attention away from ourselves? Why has God preserved this scenario all these years? These are questions that plagued my mind and made me wonder why God would direct Ahab's thoughts to a man's control rather than God's control. Perhaps there was a need for Ahab to fixate on Elijah rather than looking to God himself as the One who would bring the rain. Is there a need for some people to look to and see a man rather than God? These were questions that followed me that first week of class. Faith is invisible. Those without faith are not able to see the supernatural but need to see the concrete (humans); they need to see through the eyes of those who do have faith.

This was a personal revelation. I had been under a thwarted perception of faith as something for the benefit of my own personal relationship with God and not necessarily for the benefit of others. I had always understood that the actions of my faith were meant to help others but that others needed to hear the Word themselves. Knowing that we all need to look to Christ as our example, I hadn't considered others looking to man—or worse still, to me—for their example of godliness. I missed the verse in Colossians 1:15 that tells us that Christ is the "visible image of the invisible God." This made me wonder more about this God who would submit himself to us for his own manifestation.

God was doing something in Ahab's life to prepare him for a

faith experience, but God was also doing something in Elijah's life: building a testimony. Elijah had definitely challenged the multitude of Ahab's gods to a match. If Elijah had said, "no rain until God says" that could have been perceived as no more than what any of the other false gods presented. Remember, this was a time in history when many false gods were worshipped, idolized with memorabilia, and considered a normal way of life. What was one more god? Ahab first had to have his eyes opened to earthly power in Elijah before he was ready to experience the real power of the one true God.

After Elijah's provoking declaration, God directs him to go away and hide himself. Whoa! It would scare me if God said I had to hide. Have I ever considered that God would tell me to go away from someplace and to stay away, out of touch, and hidden? I would have a choice, just as Elijah did. Would I go and trust God that this was his purpose for something unknown to me? Would I see the invitation from God to get away from people and trust him?

A test like this came for me the first time I left home for a conference after Ron's death. The conference came in the middle of an extremely cold January. My flight was due to leave at 6:00 a.m., which meant leaving the house at 3:00 a.m. for the hour drive to the airport. Weeks before, I had been confronted with the reality that I had no one left at home to call and inform about my arrival. My three sisters and their spouses all came to dinner and discussed options, with some disapproving remarks or genuine lack of understanding for my choice to travel.

It was agreed that I would call one sister, a nurse who would be getting off the night shift, as I was boarding. I did this, got on the plane, and sat at the end of the runway until the pilot apologized that we would need to go back to the gate for de-icing. You could hear mumbling and snickers across the plane. We returned, de-iced, and again sat at the end of the runway until, for the second time, the pilot announced we would have to go back for more de-icing. You could hear the rustle of papers as people began checking their connecting flights and talking quietly amongst themselves. When we finally arrived in Dallas, I literally ran to the gate indicated on my ticket for my connecting flight. When I arrived at the gate, breathless and totally overheated in my boots, winter jacket, and gloves, there was no plane. After inquiring, I realized I had to head all the way back to my original gate. I ran all the way back to find the door closed. I pleaded with the staff, but they would not let me board the plane. Instead, they gave me a lunch ticket and a seat on the next flight.

I was a baby. I had a tantrum. Finally, I went into a restaurant near my departure gate, wedged myself between tables to sit with my back to the wall, pulled my suitcase in between the tables, and made my little cubby. After ordering, I glanced out at the main walkway and saw someone who looked just like an uncle from Indiana, whom I hadn't seen in years. If I had been in the walkway, I would have stopped this man, perhaps making a fool of myself if it wasn't him. Awaiting my lunch, I called my mom and told her about seeing this look-alike. She checked with his wife and, sure enough, he was going from California through Dallas to Indiana, and I was going from Connecticut through Dallas to Colorado. Although I heard my mom still talking to me on the phone, I heard the Lord, *You go where I tell you to go; I can put your family there if you need them.* Although I didn't speak with my uncle at that time, even in remembering that experience, I am amazed at God's purpose in my uncle's life to build up my faith. God is trustworthy to care for us and even to bring others to us as an assurance of his love.

But for Elijah, this was a time of aloneness with God, himself, and the birds. This was a refuge at a place of running water and a place where he was fed by birds that had been commanded by God. Do you ever consider that the birds' beautiful songs or that the design of the birds in flight have been commanded by God for you? I love the early, pre-dawn hours on the back-porch stoop, where even seconds can change the color of the sky. I have always considered the beauty of those sunrises to be a gift from God, as he knows how much I appreciate beauty, and a refuge where I can spend time alone with him.

Did Elijah spend his time thinking about other stories of running water? It reminds me of Moses striking the rock in Numbers 20:11, manna from heaven in Exodus 16:4, or the quail in Exodus 16:13. Perhaps this is a prophetic picture of Christ identifying himself as "the living water." We may never know what was being revealed to Elijah in that time of solitude. That is his story, but these questions made him real to me.

A point comes (1 Kings 17:7), *after a while*, where the brook dries up because of his own words and Elijah has to move on. We don't know how long that time took. It may have been three days; it may have been three months. Now Elijah gets to experience the consequences of his words that others were already experiencing: his brook dried up. He has no water. He experiences thirst.

There is so much that can be said about the consequences of our own words, but this was an example of prophetic irony. As we consider the situation, we read in verse 7 that though Elijah could see the brook drying up, he still remained until God gave the direction. The reality from a human perspective is that Elijah didn't have to go to the brook to begin with, and he could have left whenever he chose. But please notice that God didn't speak until the necessity arose. God designs the time of our rest. God is the One who determines the length of our time with him.

God was giving Elijah a new vision—a forward look, a milestone, an end to one chapter and an anticipation of something positive rather than drought, King Ahab, and his stubbornness. God determined the time of rest and reflection, and he determined the end of it. God was pointing Elijah's thinking to someone else, someone new. God was planting in Elijah's heart a vision of provision, of food and relationship. God gave it in a time of need. Verse 7 says, "after a while the brook dried up." Again, this was God's timing and the economy of it. Remember that in Revelation 3:11

and 22:20, Jesus says that he is coming soon, and that was two thousand years ago.

Dear widow, have you experienced a time of aloneness? Can you look back on a time when your basic needs were being met, but you were alone? Did you spend time alone with God? Are you there now? Re-read your journals or take the time to now journal the provision given to you during that time. Thank him for what he is giving you today. For me, there was a year of meeting the dawn, up between 4:00 a.m. and 7:30 a.m., alone every morning on the back stoop. I just sat and waited. No one else was awake; there was no ringing phone to distract me, just the early morning sounds of earth.

At that time, I didn't see my year of sunrises as preparation; I saw it as peace. But looking back, I can see that it was also a year of learning to identify God's goodness to me in the people and ways he provided.

chapter eight

A STUDY IN PREPARATION—
BOTH ELIJAH AND THE WIDOW

Then the word of the LORD came to him, saying: "Arise,
go to Zarephath, which belongs to Sidon, and dwell there.
See, I have commanded a widow there to provide for
you." So he arose and went to Zarephath.
1 Kings 17:8 NKJV

THIS PASSAGE BEGINS WITH instructions: "Arise." This statement implies both physical and emotional action, indicat-
ing an end of resting time (see Joshua 1:2). The term *arise* is used
frequently to indicate a change in positioning and an end to one
phase of life.

"See, I have commanded a widow there to provide for you."
The word *see* is the Hebrew word *hinnêh*, which means: "Lo!, behold, see [from the primary particle expressing surprise]."[7] Old En-
glish might have said, "Alas!" Today we might say, "Hey look!" In

---

[7] R. Laird Harris, Gleason L. Archer Jr., Bruce K. Waltke, *Theological Word Book*
of the Old Testament, featuring words found in *Brown, Driver, Briggs Hebrew*
Lexicon, keyed to *Strong's Concordance* (Moody Publishers, 1980).

other words, the first recorded word from God to Elijah was one to catch his attention.

The vast ways God can get our attention are as numerous and different as snowflakes. Think of the times you've experienced a near miss on the roadways, found money that had been forgotten, or had a random thought that took you back to the house to avert a problem. If, instead, we consider these things as God protecting us from a wrong turn or guiding us through something new, we will begin to grow in the knowledge of God's love for us.

What are some ways you can see circumstances that you may have considered good luck, when in reality God may have been giving you a *behold* moment?

We will consider what this meant for the widow in our story later. What did this mean to Elijah? Was he a single man who waited for a wife? Was he an abused, neglected child who needed a mom, or was he a man of obedience to the Lord in spite of the appearances of approaching a single woman—a widow?

When the Lord says, "I have commanded," in Scripture, he is communicating that he is in charge, he has provided, and that he will still provide by commanding others to care for you. This infers the obedient spirit of another person. When Elijah was feeling alone, isolated, and hidden from other human relationships, God relays the information that there is another human being obedient to His commands—a widow.

Who is this widow that God would use her to minister to a minister? Exactly how desperate would one have to be to rationally prepare a last meal before death? This level of resignation to life circumstances is unknown in our society. We hear of seasons of drought in our nation that last two or three years and cause a loss of grain, but our loss doesn't hit us immediately; prices are raised, and after a while, we eat a little less. Our global society, which knows of problems across the world and arranges food drops, can't really appreciate the level of this widow's hopelessness. In this story, the food is completely gone. She was living day by day, meal by meal, and moment by moment. She was dependent. She was hopeless. She was without the living God.

I wonder what life experiences God fashioned for her to bring her to that point of acceptance, or what difficulties prepared her for what was to come. She was a Gentile woman living under a king who "did evil in the sight of the Lord" (1 Kings 16:30 NKJV), who denied the God of Abraham, Isaac, and Jacob. Her statement in verse 12 acknowledges that Elijah's God was his and not hers. I wonder if she had heard of the Law or of the history of Israel and judgments through drought (Deut. 28:24). Her society was one of apostasy under Ahab, but was all morality gone?

What about her husband's brothers or her own family? Was it socially acceptable to have a man and an outsider as provider? How did she explain the man in her house to her neighbors, to her family, to her son, or to herself? Were there no neighbors to see? Was she so destitute that cultural mores had no meaning? She had lost everything except her child, her life, a handful of flour, and a little oil. We may never know her level of hopelessness expressed in her statement: "I am gathering sticks that I may go in and prepare it for myself and my son, that we may eat it and die," or the level of intimacy God poured into her before she met the prophet. That is her story.

In today's world, we may never experience this type of life or death challenge. The love gift of God is that we each have our own individual testings. We do not live in her time or culture; we do not know her heart. Only God knows our hearts. We cannot judge her, only grow in our understanding of God's love for her and for each of us. He included her in a story that is thousands of years old, and we are reading about her today! Our testings with cultural mores may be more subtle. Do we stay in the prayer room alone with a married man in spite of each being there for prayer? Do we drive our own car rather than ride alone with a man? Do we stay in work situations that present the appearance of inappropriate intimacy to others, which might require late-night meetings or dinners out with others? As God's special possessions, how do we live above reproach? Do you see yourself as God's special possession?

Who is this God who protects a widow—at the point of death—cares for Elijah with birds, and brings these two characters together? Can we figure out God? No. Can we trust him? Yes. Does he deliver? Yes! David says in 2 Samuel 22: 2–3: "The Lord is my rock, my fortress, and my savior; my God is my rock, in whom I find protection. He is my shield, the power that saves me, and my place of safety. He is my refuge, my savior, the one who saves me from violence."

Both the widow and Elijah were coming from spaces of aloneness with God. Both were coming from different, difficult pasts. Hunger for human connection happens in solitude, which leads to risk taking. Inner trust also happens in solitude. Each had a specific assignment from God that would show forth his glory to the generations. The widow was a worker who went about her daily work gathering sticks for a fire, expressed kindness to go for water, spoke respect for Elijah and his God, humbled herself under his instruction, and had some measure of hunger for the true God—all actions and characteristics of good leadership.

Elijah was a prophet with a word and a miracle to demonstrate God's grace. Both the widow and Elijah contributed to an expression of God's character. Each was growing in intimacy with God. That intimacy was the preparation for what was to come.

Long before my husband took sick, he had been known to snore loudly. At a men's retreat, they dubbed him the snorasaurus. I had struggled with his snoring too, and in response, I began using ear buds to listen to Scripture through the night. I would often fall asleep, only to awaken in the morning and go search out Scripture I'd heard during the night that had somehow stuck with me. I believe that this nightly infusion of Scripture began a deep intimacy with God that went beyond anything I could have done myself to attain intimacy.

Some develop intimacy through reading the Bible. One way

to start is by reading five psalms and one proverb daily. Another method is to use *The One Year Bible.* Each of these practices takes about fifteen minutes and can jump-start your thought life. His presence, revelation, and timing are out of this world! You may be busy, overworked, or overwhelmed, but you will have a much better day if you give God the first part of it. Preparation is the key; prepare to sit quietly to wait on God, and keep your Bible, paper, and pen nearby to write down all the tasks or worries that try to steal the beauty of your quietness with him. When you write down your distractions, it frees your mind to focus on God, knowing your tasks are in an orderly place.

Genesis 1:5 says, "Evening passed and the morning came, marking the first day." This made me reflect on how I look at my day. If my day "started" in the evening, what would that mean? For me, it changed my life. As best I am able, I evaluate my calendar for what is to come: I prepare my clothes, my lunch, and all the things that need to go to work the evening before my day. My Bible, journal, and notepad are in their place, the coffeepot is ready, and I sleep well, not letting the burden of those responsibilities carry over into my thought life for the night. This preparation sets the pace for quiet time with Jesus. This is how God has brought order to my days.

God is always working toward relationship. His desire is for intimacy with his created, with each one of us. We are created in his image, so we have that same desire for intimacy. When we put him first, he works even through our good, bad, and ugly. Dearest widow, how has God been calling you into a relationship of intimacy with him? Have you considered yourself the bride of Christ, not just in the spiritual connotation but in earthly reality? What are the challenges that your social standards impose? As a married-to-Christ woman, what are the challenges that your social mores impose? How can you restructure your day to include more quiet time for reading the Bible and for listening to God? Write down your thoughts and your questions, and ask God to reveal his answers and himself to you. Look for Scriptures that can strengthen your faith in God and convict you that he loves you in a way no human can.

Pastors and leaders, trusting that you have already developed an intimacy with Christ, how do you refresh yourselves in him daily? Reflect on the time of preparation God had for you. Have you ever inadvertently positioned widows where compromise would be possible? If so, how can you address that? Do you see each widow as a married bride, precious to Christ? How do you live above reproach? Do you always counsel women with another woman in the room? While shepherding widows, do you encourage them to depend on God rather than on man?

God is calling his bride, the church, to a higher standard of living than any social norms could match. As we immerse ourselves in him, we can trust him to guide us.

chapter nine

LOSS OF EXPECTATION

*Loss, whether expected or unexpected,
touches on every other unresolved loss within.*
—Mary Bruce

SOMETIMES LOSS OF AN expectation is more difficult to deal with than actual loss of something physical. Loss of an expectation is invisible, a subconscious event. We all experience expectations: we expect the parking garage arm to stay up until we are through, we expect the bus to run on time, we expect the weatherman to be wrong, we expect the alarm to wake us up. We basically live our lives on expectations.

Expectations are what newly-married couples spend their first year realizing. She says she'll be right there, and ten minutes later he's still waiting. Now they're late for that business dinner with his boss, and there's heaviness for the evening. He says he'll be home by 5:30, the soufflé is right on time, the company arrives at 5:20, and he doesn't show up until 6:00! Now the salad is wilted, dinner is dry, and the wife is learning a life lesson in front of company. The use of time takes on a new meaning. The joke about who squeezes the toothpaste from what end is standard cover-up for the hardship of learning to live a daily life with someone else. Unconscious expectations are being worked through.

We spend years during childhood developing expectations of dependence on someone else. Then we get to grow up. This is basically known as the teen struggle for independence and identity. For many of us, once through those tumultuous teen years, adulthood allows total self-absorption, the ability to live completely for ourselves: my schooling, my car, my apartment, etc. However in this broken world, we have people who may have not completed that struggle for independence in their teen years, so they carry the invisible, continual search for independence and identity into their adult years. This is the perfect setup for unconscious expectations. In brokenness, it's easy to transfer dependency on another person when that search for identity has not been fulfilled. Dependency is another aspect of expectations.

When I was young, children were expected to be seen and not heard, polite, and respectful of elders. Young girls were to finish high school, get some useful education, then get married, have children, and be content raising a family. Young men were expected to enter the military, go to college or trade school, and avoid marriage as long as possible before settling down and becoming happy as the breadwinner and head of the home.

I fell into that trap of pre-determined expectations. After marriage, when plans didn't go as expected and we were unable to conceive, we set off for sunny Florida, settling in Miami. Our home was about twenty miles west of the actual city where we both worked. Because my shift started and finished early, I usually arrived home first. There were occasions when Ron would arrive home later than usual. Between his expected and actual time home, I would work myself into a panic frenzy of "what ifs." *What if he had an accident? What if he was in such a big wreck that the police can't identify him? What if he was attacked in the inner city on his way to the car? What if he has a girlfriend?* And the list went on and on.

I'm sorry to say that my attitude upon his arrival in these situations was often one of hostility, mistrust, and loss of expectation. It was one of those nights, however, that drove me to the floor before the King of heaven and brought me to a decision about my own life. Ron's absence touched on my own unresolved abandonment issues and my immature dependency. I experienced a loss of expectation. Ron had met all the criteria of my youthful expectations, and an imaginary loss through some freak accident was too much to bear. As I lay on the floor, in my utter sense of abandonment, God reached down to show me his mercy. I surrendered to God as Lord of my life. Within ten minutes, Ron came through the door, soiled and messy. He'd had a flat tire on the four-lane highway and changed it himself.

I wish I could say that surrendering to God or knowing that the delay was due only to a flat tire rid me of my imagination and abandonment issues. It didn't. I still entered my panic zone when worrying that he might not get home. Years later, I overheard him explaining the items in the trunk of his car to someone. He carried extra supplies because he loved to stop whenever anyone had a flat tire to offer help and open doors to spiritual conversations. Had I realized that he was on a God-assignment all those times, I may have responded differently, and there would have been fewer expectations on him and more on the Lord. I like to think I may have prayed: *God, what do you have for Ron in these minutes?* I might have greeted Ron with eager anticipation, rather than anger or sullenness. Hindsight is always easy.

Jeremiah 17:7 says, "But blessed are those who trust in the LORD and have made the LORD their hope and confidence." Lamentations 3:24 also speaks of putting our hope in God: "I say to myself, 'The LORD is my inheritance; therefore, I will hope in him!'" Loss of expectation can produce pressure that either drives us to the Lord or away from the Lord. I had been such a whimpering baby in those moments with Ron. Yet, they were the beginnings of putting my expectations on God.

As tough as life had already been, Elijah was about to experience a loss of expectation. Elijah was not the only prophet in hiding; Jezebel was on a rampage, massacring the prophets of the Lord (1 Kings 18:4). Elijah had been safely hidden and provided for divinely. The command was now: "Arise, go to Zarephath, which belongs to Sidon, and stay there" (1 Kings 17:9 NASB).

Zarephath was nearly one hundred miles away in Sidon, Samaria, the childhood homeland of Jezebel before her marriage to Ahab. This was the geographical birthplace of the Baal worship of Jezebel and Ahab. After his time in hiding, Elijah walked from the frying pan into the fire. We don't know how long it took for the brook to dry up. After living alone, Elijah knew that God could be trusted as Jehovah-Jireh—provider—and Jehovah-Nissi—protector. God had already said, "I have commanded a widow there to provide for you" (1 Kings 17:9 NASB). Consider your own thoughts if you had to walk one hundred miles to the place where your enemy was born and raised. Jezebel and Ahab were still prowling the land to find prophets.

We may never know Elijah's thoughts on that long walk. His physical difficulties, hunger, and thirst are not described, nor considered significant by God to set in history. Sure enough, as Elijah approached the city, he found the widow God has prepared for him. He initiated the relationship with a request for one of the most treasured commodities: a little water in a cup. Her response: to go to get it. I can just imagine Elijah thinking, *Yes, this is the one commanded by God to provide for me. No more bird food; real home cooking is coming my way!*

The story continues in verses 11 and 12: "As she was going to get it, he called to her and said, 'Please bring me a piece of bread in your hand.' But she said, 'As the LORD your God lives, I have no bread, only a handful of flour in the bowl and a little oil in the jar; and behold, I am gathering a few sticks that I may go in and prepare it for me and my son, that we may eat it and die.'" Talk about loss of expectation: all that Elijah has to look at is a little cake. Both Elijah and the widow were still in learning mode, learning Yahweh's ways. As you are confronted with situations that seem hopeless, entrust yourself to God who judges justly, according to 1 Peter 2:23. If you look, you will see that Elijah's relationship with this widow provided lessons in tithing (give first to the Lord), deliverance from famine, activation of faith, and knowledge of the one true God.

Just like this widow, your personal growth through expectations may contribute to someone else's faith walk in the future. We are still today learning about faith through the example of this widow.

chapter ten

WHAT'S IN A NAME?—
BAAL OR ISHI

See how very much our Father loves us,
for he calls us his children, and that is what we are!
1 John 3:1

A T ONE NEW HAMPSHIRE National Day of Prayer Training Day that I attended, Emily Gerghas, a college student in New Hampshire, gave a message entitled "What's Your Name?" She described the idea that we subconsciously call ourselves many names often based on our childhood experiences or past history. An earlier reference to this was made at the beginning of chapter 6. Things others have said to us or about us can penetrate deeply and cause either positive or negative perceptions of ourselves. Some of my names have been given to me by children and caused me to want to live up to those name. Many times, we call ourselves names based on our roles: mom, nurse, wife, chauffeur, etc. These are titles we consciously and subconsciously call ourselves during the course of a day. Emily challenged us to spend a little time thinking about what name we call ourselves by the end of each day, when we lay our head on the pillow.

Identity was not a big topic years ago. Today there are thousands of books listed online with titles that include the word *identity*. Why? Could it be that by removing God from secular culture we have denied our younger ones their identity and purpose? Broken families have resulted in broken people. "Made in God's image" has been replaced by Darwinism, and "made for God's purpose" has been replaced by "whatever makes you happy and doesn't hurt someone else," a setup for rebellion and complete chaos. Young people can identify with the role of child, student, or sibling, yet without knowing God's purpose for their lives, they will often believe the value or lack of value imposed by their peers. This thinking has prevailed for more than fifty years in our nation. Consequently, we are surrounded by generations who do not have a sense of worth or an understanding of God's value on their lives.

Here are some of the names God calls us in his Word:

1. Children of God. "But as many as received Him, to them He gave the right to become children of God, even to those who believe in his name" (John 1:12 NASB).
2. Joint heirs with Christ. "The Spirit Himself bears witness with our spirit that we are children of God, and if children, then heirs—joint heirs with Christ" (Rom. 8:16–17 NKJV).
3. Blessed. "More than that, blessed are those who hear the word of God and keep it" (Luke 11:28 NKJV).
4. Beloved. "To the praise of the glory of His grace, by which He made us accepted in the Beloved" (Ephesians 1:6).

You can probably think of many more that are favorites to you. Write them in the margin and quote them to yourself. Pastor Brian Simmons, author of *The Passion Translation*, who has visited my local church several times, suggests we speak the character of God over ourselves and pray for whichever of God's character traits we desire the most to be perfected in us. I did this for years, daily wearing a small bead bracelet with the word *gentleness* on it. My communication style, developed through my nursing profession, was very direct, which aided in successful problem solving, but was often interpreted as bossy and short-tempered. I needed gentleness and wore that bracelet as a reminder.

God has a specific purpose for you in your widowhood, and it isn't all about you. Years after giving up the bracelet, it was a great delight to hear myself being described as gentle and to be told that some aspired to be gentle like me. See that he is perfecting others through you and your circumstances. Your children may be learning piety through your difficulties. First Timothy 5:4 (NASB) says, "But if any widow has children or grandchildren, they must first learn to practice piety in regard to their own family and to make some return to their parents; for this is acceptable in the sight of God." Newer widows will be looking to you, and you will be able to comfort others. Second Corinthians 1:3–4 (NASB) says, "Blessed be the God and Father of our Lord Jesus Christ, the Father of mercies and God of all comfort, who comforts us in all our affliction so that we will be able to comfort those who are in any affliction with the comfort with which we ourselves are comforted by God."

By acknowledging the name *widow*, you will give others opportunity to obey the Lord and to receive his peace: "For if you truly amend your ways and your deeds, if you truly practice justice between a man and his neighbor, if you do not oppress the alien, the orphan, or the widow, and do not shed innocent blood in this place, nor walk after other gods to your own ruin, then I will let you dwell in this place, in the land that I gave to your fathers forever and ever" (Jer. 7:5–7 NASB).

So what's in a name? By what name do you call God? What's your favorite name for him? Do you see God as the father, husband, or bridegroom? I think this is different for every widow yearning to know God, however, stumbling blocks can hinder the reality of our God's loving intention for us. One such stumbling block for me was a misunderstanding of Scripture.

In Old Testament times, the term *baal* was used as a regular word for "husband" or "master." It was also the name of a Canaanite false god. Because so many identified it as a false god, and because it was used to describe ownership rather than relationship, God chose to refer to himself as Ishi. Ishi, another term that means husband, is the term God used to mean a loving husband, rather than master of a slave. What Scripture meant about the nation of Israel, I applied literally to myself because it was associated with the term widow.

Chapters 49–54 of Isaiah describe God's redeeming hope for Israel and for all nations (Isa. 49:6). Marriage is one figure of speech used to relate God's desire for Israel. Israel's sins and desire for comforts, deliverance, and corrections—brought through other nations—promised by God, reveal the Father's persistent love and faithfulness to his Word.

Isaiah 54:3–5 (NASB) reads, "For you will spread abroad to the right and to the left. And your descendants will possess nations and will resettle the desolate cities. 'Fear not, for you will not be put to shame; and do not feel humiliated, for you will not be disgraced; but you will forget the shame of your youth, and the *reproach of your widowhood you will remember no more.* For your husband is your Maker, whose name is the LORD of hosts; and your Redeemer is the Holy One of Israel, who is called the God of all the earth.'" This is referring to the nation of Israel and the putting away of its former griefs. God draws them back through a wilderness where he can speak comfort to them in isolation. Hosea 2:14–20 (NKJV) describes God giving Israel a door of hope, a Valley of Achor. In verse 14, he says, "I will allure her, will bring her into the wilderness, and speak comfort to her."

For many years I stumbled and saw my name as *reproach.* I often associated every mistake (especially financial), overlooked calendar items, and failures to meet self-imposed timelines as part of the reproach of widowhood. My problem was that I got stuck in the concept of reproach of widowhood without understanding the true context of the passage. Reproach stuck with me for nearly ten years. The word reproach infers disappointment or disapproval. The years of misunderstanding plummeted me into striving to make up for whatever was worthy of disapproval. My hard work was often efforts to justify my existence, in spite of what I considered to be God's disapproval of something in me. Although my morning retreats with the Lord continued, and I had great blessings in them, I began to question his intentions for me in church, in ministry, and in all my activities. This brought a whole gamut of negative, wrong thoughts that became stumbling blocks and contributed to a victim mentality, rather than a privileged-calling mentality. Joseph Benson's *Commentary on the Old and New Testament* clarifies Isaiah 54:3–5 with the understanding that God is saying the people of Israel will "no longer feel disconsolate, deprived or forsaken,"[8] which are all feelings that a widow could have. To outsiders, and to us personally, we can use our circumstances to be a time of feeling forsaken or without consolation, or we can use our situation to cry out to God and grow in intimacy with him. Every crisis is an opportunity. In this case, besides taking my own literal interpretation, I neglected the end of the sentence in Isaiah 54:4: *you will remember no more.*

There are times when *remembering no more* could be related to a more comical side of my situation. After Ron died, it was three months before I ran out of toilet tissue, and I found myself unsure if it was a product to be purchased at Staples or at the grocery store; he had done the grocery shopping. Then there were the three frying pans I burned to a crisp and had to throw away, the two times I pulled away from the gas pump without disconnecting the hose, the time I wore a new dress to church with the size ticket hanging off the back, the year of sleeping in a sleeping bag because it reminded me of our camping times together, and the daily cans of

---

[8] Joseph Benson, *Commentary on the Old and New Testament* (Originally published by G. Lane & C. B. Tippett, 1845), Kindle version (Patristic Publishing, 2019).

tuna I forced myself to eat in remembrance of a man who loved it. Were these all things I needed to remember no more?

One thing that provoked change for me more than anything else was the verse from Hosea 2:14. Truthfully, it is only God's Spirit who can change us. Perhaps it was just time to change my thinking and claim my marriage to Ishi.

In Hosea 2:14, the word *allure* stuck out. I thought about a fishing lure and the process of threading it, casting out, and carefully bringing that lure through the water with sensitive hands to sense the smallest nudge. I recognized the Lord alluring me, tenderly drawing me to himself, waiting for my response, and I was hooked! Meditating on that verse was my aha moment in understanding a deeper love of God. The Lord will be your husband. Isaiah 54:5 (NASB) says, "For your husband is your Maker, whose name is the LORD of hosts; and your Redeemer is the Holy One of Israel, who is called the God of all the earth."

What character trait is God perfecting in you through your circumstance, your interactions with others, and your own relationship with him? Ask what he wants to perfect in and through you for your family, for those you lead, for yourself, and for his pleasure. Is there an area of obedience God is asking of you, such as was asked of the widow in 1 Kings 17? Can you see his direction in 1 Timothy 5:5? How was the widow's faith and humility in 2 Kings 4:1–7 an example to her children and neighbors? Jesus has compassion for you. Read Luke 7:11–17. God is building a wonderful picture of his love for you through your difficulties.

chapter eleven

A NEW BRIDAL VEIL

*Therefore, behold, I [the Lord] will allure her [Israel], will
bring her into the wilderness and speak comfort to her. I
will give her vineyards from there, and the Valley of Achor
as a door of hope; she shall sing there. As in the days of her
youth, as in the day when she came up from the land of
Egypt. "And it shall be, in that day," says the LORD, "that
you will call Me 'My Husband,' and no longer call Me
'My Master.'"*

Hosea 2:14–16 NKJV

To: Linda
From: Mary Sent: Sat, 25 Apr 2009 12:43 pm
Subject: question
Hi Linda,
I meant to speak with you before you left regarding a
prayer shawl from Israel. I have such a yearning for a
prayer shawl. I don't know why this is significant to me,
and I do believe that I will someday step there with my
own two feet, but for some reason, I sense a need for one
now. I have purchased one, but it doesn't seem right,
and I haven't used it, will probably give it to another. I

would like one that I know has come from Jerusalem, even possibly been opened and used at the wailing wall, been rubbed in the dirt of the land . . . is that weird? You know many people who come and go from there. Can you help me with this heart desire?

Date: Sat, 25 Apr 2009 13:58:16–0400
To: unknown
From: Linda
Subject: prayer shawl
Greetings. Please read the following from a dear intercessor friend of mine, Mary ☺
Is there any possibility that you might could help out with a prayer shawl? If so, let me know blessings, Linda

It was not so bizarre to awaken one Saturday morning with the need for a prayer shawl in my thoughts. What was bizarre was that I actually went to the computer and acted upon it and am amazed at the rapidity with which my request went around the world. Within eight minutes of Linda's response to my email, I started receiving answers, comments, and apologies from those with whom Linda connected. I received messages from as far as Texas and London. It was exciting to think that others from all over the world were thinking of something I had asked about.

The idea of a prayer shawl was not new to me. I have my Mexican rebozo that I use often in my own prayer time. Actually, I had used a Jewish prayer shawl that belonged to a new state coordinator a few weeks earlier in a commissioning ceremony. Following the model of Numbers 27:22–23, in which Moses is told to commission and to give some of his spiritual authority to Joshua, I had previously used a prayer shawl as a visual teaching tool before congregations.

The morning after my inquiry for the prayer shawl, we had a special ministry speaker at church from Florida. The speaker had a huge banner and flags presentation. It was a beautiful design of worship, new to my thinking. That evening, he used another banner with the Star of David on it as well as a cross. He explained that while at the Wailing Wall in Israel, someone had tried to destroy the banner because it included both symbols. That person had grabbed the banner and actually torn part of it and gotten dirt on it before it was reclaimed by the ministry team. I thought: *Wow! This must be what I was seeing in my dreams.* I reveled at how God can show us things before they happen.

On Monday, as I was driving home from work, I received a call from my friend Linda. She was laughing and telling me about an email that had just come through. Did I know who Rosemary was?

> To: Linda, "Rosemary"
> From: Marcelyn
> Date: Monday, April 27, 2009, 9:50 AM
> Rosemary—This is a dear friend of ours who has worked with us with Bobbie and now assigned as an intercessor and works with the government and with Sara . . . Her friend needs your shawl!!! :-)Linda—Rosemary is en route to an assignment/invite by the German Govt.—will land and change planes in a couple hours! Blessings! Love in Yeshua, Marcelyn

I did not know Marcelyn or Rosemary, but later spoke with Rosemary Schindler. Rosemary is keeper of the flame for her uncle, Oskar Schindler, who saved the lives of many Jewish workers during the Nazi persecution in Poland. Rosemary is the family representative to nations. She resides in California and travels, taking others to Israel. She was approached by some Jewish women while in Israel the previous January. They told her that the Lord told them to make prayer shawls for American prayer-warrior women and asked her to take them to America. Rosemary didn't know which prayer warriors the shawls were intended for, but she obeyed the Spirit and agreed. Here I was, a prayer warrior, asking for a prayer shawl four months later.

I left the decision to Rosemary about which shawl to send. After all, what I had already experienced through following this desire had been supplied in just hearing from Rosemary. What an encouragement to her and to me. Whatever shawl arrived would matter less than the remembrance of how God was connecting me with Israel.

The prayer shawl arrived a short while later. I had hoped for an everyday piece of fabric that had touched the Wailing Wall and might have a little Jerusalem dirt on it. Instead, the shawl that arrived was a beautiful bridal shawl. I was overwhelmed by its beauty and showed it off to everybody. I prayed over it and dedicated it to the Lord, but I only used it as a prayer shawl in my private space, thinking it way too beautiful to use in public. I did not know the extent of God's love for me in this way.

It has taken years for me to see myself in this shawl. Through the years, I've seen God supply my needs, protect me through travels, and bring others around to care for me and provide fellowship. Under the leading of my pastor in my local church, I've taken several personality tests and have been given greater responsibility within the congregation. God has allowed me to persevere through transitions in my family life and living circumstances as well as in ministry. Now I know that wearing the bridal shawl is representative of what Christ does to sanctify his people. I was so consumed with being a physical widow, that regardless of my words about God as my husband, my heart saw only this physical realm and not what Christ was doing in my spirit realm. Recently, I began an in-depth study of Revelation, a book all about the bride (church) and the bridegroom (Christ). The study has helped me to more clearly understand God's perspective on Israel as the nation through which he has chosen to demonstrate his character. I see myself more as part of the church and less as a lone widow. The tearing of the relationship with my husband is being mended by the body of Christ, the church at large. Now, when I'm prompted to wear this beautiful garment, it's not for me but for Christ, my Ishi.

chapter twelve

LIVING IN THE REST
OF MY LIFE

G OD LOVES AND HONORS widows. There are many places in Scripture where God cares for and defends widows, tells others to take care of them, and speaks of punishment for those who cause them harm. A widow who has read to this point may feel as if she is too overwhelmed to put any positive steps into practice and that life is too hard without her husband. Truthfully, no one can replace your husband. You may think a new life mate will help, and that may be true. However during your widowhood, God desires to fill this void for you. In Matthew 11:28–29 (NKJV), Jesus says, "Come to Me, all you who labor and are heavy laden, and I will give you rest. Take my yoke upon you and learn from me, for I am gentle and lowly in heart, and you will find rest for your souls." This is not specifically for widows but for all people. Rest is not just something that comes with sleep. Rest includes a sense of not being alone, especially in the work of life. Being yoked is an old farming term related to partnering two oxen together with a wooden yoke.

Oxen of similar size would be yoked together so that they could pace together. Jesus offers himself as the other partner for your empty yoke. This is living in his rest.

By reading stories of biblical widows, we can strengthen our knowledge of God's love. When we hear the redemptive stories of widows today, we can grow in faith that God will take care of us. Relying on God moment by moment can become the doorway to a significant relationship with Christ.

Personally, God has met me in my deepest insecurities, in my awkward moments of aloneness, in my saddest memories, and in my silliest times. I've had opportunities to ask forgiveness for ways I've offended others, to forgive others for ways they have offended me, to share deep questions with men and women of faith, and to appreciate the creativity of God in the variety of human beings I've encountered. As I speak with other widows, I see them reflecting different aspects of God's character; I see his development of leadership within them in each of their life situations.

Regardless of how old a woman is when she becomes a widow, there is a sisterhood with others who have come through the experience. In a way, it's like parenting: when a new parent is speaking about some first-time struggle, unless the hearer has experienced it, there's an emotional gap between what is being said about the struggle and the fullness of what is being understood. For some, our personality types and the ways in which we process trauma may keep us from tapping into that sisterhood. Every person has a unique way of coming through loss. The sisterhood is there, however, to help us develop one another and can become a pivotal place for friendship and for planting leadership seeds.

Widowhood can be a way that God works through his church, the body of Christ. In James 1:27 (NASB) we read, "Pure and undefiled religion in the sight of our God and Father is this: to visit orphans and widows in their distress, and to keep oneself unstained by the world." As a widow, you give others the opportunity to demonstrate pure and undefiled religion. One family helped me to manage my house and property for many of my early years as a widow, and they still help when I have need. This dad brought his children with him as he practiced pure and undefiled religion before not only me but also them. I had no problem sharing how much they helped me, the testimony of answered prayers through their help. Who knows how many people were affected through what I considered to be my troubles.

Recently, I received some unexpected monies, and I decided to purchase some items for a new widow. I included a dozen eggs, along with the other items. Later I received a message that she had been shopping and also thought to pick up an extra dozen eggs for me! In our conversation about the mutual exchange of eggs, she offered to help with my laundry when I'm in a crunch, since I live in an apartment with no laundry facilities. She considered it a blessing to be able to help me. This is the fellowship of Christ's body working together.

Church leaders, for widows there is that emotional gap that the church can help to fill during the consolation days of widowhood. One widow reminded me about the difficulty of losing all of her husband's friends upon his death. Keep in mind that a widow can benefit from help to make the transition from being a part of her husband's life to being a part of the church life. Find someone who can take the initiative to offer rides to the widow. Look ahead for her, and look for ways to include her in church life. If she has been an active part of the congregation, accept the fact that her role may change for a season, but that she will benefit the church body as she grows in her personal life. Help her to expect other changes in her life based on her new, head-of-household responsibilities. Help her see the love of God in all of it, and provide outlets for her to express her struggles. Find ways to help her with legal aspects of what surrounds the death of a spouse. Funeral homes, wills, transfer of titles, and probate are all cloudy subjects that a widow may need to negotiate. Encourage any widows in your congregation who have successfully managed widowhood to become mentors or to provide financial counseling, grief counseling, etc.

Dear widow, I hope that this work has helped you find comfort, a place to reflect on some of your own feelings, and a space to sharpen a restored or new vision for yourself. I pray God has affirmed for you ways in which you are a leader.

If you are a pastor and have gotten this far, I congratulate you. I understand time constraints in a busy life. I pray a new destiny for every widow that you shepherd. If you are a friend of a widow, I pray you will be a blessing for your friend to help her fulfill the destiny for her life.

author's note

FOR THE WIDOW WHO does not know of Christ. . .
As a widow who has gone through loss, I identify with you. Whether your loss has been expected or sudden, my heart goes out to you and your family, not so much in sympathy for your loss, for you may have family and friends who are helping you with that, but in sympathy for the attitude of our society and even the Christian church, which tends to feed you a victim mentality.

Biblically, women of the Middle East were generally treated as second-class citizens or even non-citizens. Their status and their worth were based upon their outward appearance or the fame of their husbands. Jesus presented a different level of respect for women. He honored them in public, and that honoring has lasted thousands of years through Scripture. He honors you today, with an invitation to something only God can give: the understanding of your true worth and a freedom to live out the fullness of what God has planned for you. It begins with honesty—you being honest with yourself and honest with God.

None of us is born perfect. We all want to do things our own way. This is how we teach children the meaning of sin. It's the attitude of: *I want to do it my way.* From the time we are born, we know how to rebel. No one has to teach the one-year-old how to keep heading to the wall plugs after being told not to. The independent desire to resist authority comes with birth. Just as your blue eyes or brown hair came to you through your ancestors, so also comes the desire to do things your own way. Being honest with God is admitting that desire, seeing how that desire has failed to give you inner peace, recognizing you cannot earn heaven, and humbling yourself to invite Jesus into your life to make payment for your sins.

If the snapshot of your life right now includes undesirable thoughts, feelings, or actions, you may need a new method of dealing with life and a new way of communicating. You may need non-chemical, non-alcoholic, non-denial help—a new kind of help. Jesus is the help you need. His new commandment to the world was to love one another. He is love, he knows everything, and he cares for you individually. Negative thoughts, feelings, or actions may paint a different picture of God. Circumstances and people change. History of the Triune God written in the Bible is thousands of years old and hasn't changed. He is and always will be the God of love.

You have a choice. You can believe the negative things you see in the world with your eyes, or you can make a decision to believe the invisible love of God. He depends on people to make his love visible, and there are many who are working to do that.

If your choice is to invite Jesus into your life, you can do that where you are. He is all-knowing and recognizes your intention. Just ask Jesus to forgive you for wanting to be the one in charge of your life and for your own sinfulness. Invite him to come into your life and to be in charge of you. As you truthfully do this, you will be blessed with his peace and his Holy Spirit who will direct you. You are not alone. He will be with you. Get ready! He is an adventurer!

If you have prayed to invite Jesus to be in charge of your life, please tell someone. No doubt, you can recognize someone who has been praying for you or talking to you about God. I am praying that you will find a community of believers in Jesus who can help you walk out your new faith in Christ. This is important: find some who can affirm your decision and challenge you. Get a Bible and begin reading Psalms and the Gospel of John. You will be blessed.

appendix A

ADDITIONAL RESOURCES

For Widows:

Dave and Jan Dravecky, *Do Not Lose Heart* (Zondervan, 1998).

Alice Gray, *Stories for the Faithful Heart* (Multnomah Publishers, 2000).

Miriam Neff, *From One Widow to Another* (Moody Publishers, 2009).

For Widowers:

Jerry Sittser, *A Grace Disguised* (Zondervan, 1995).

appendix B

BENEFITS OF WIDOWHOOD

FOLLOWING IS A LIST of ten benefits of being a widow. Feel free to copy it, display it, and share it to encourage yourself and remind you of the blessings that come with this calling.

TEN BENEFITS
OF BEING A WIDOW

1. The Lord is your husband. (Isaiah 54:5)

2. The Lord will establish your boundaries and protect you. (Proverbs 15:25)

3. The Lord will hear your cry. (Exodus 22:22–23)

4. The Lord will be your relief. (Psalm 146:9)

5. You will give others opportunity to obey the Lord and to receive his peace. (Jeremiah 7:5–7)

6. Your children will learn piety at home. (1 Timothy 5:4)

7. You will give others opportunity to demonstrate pure religion. (James 1:27)

8. You will be able to comfort others. (2 Corinthians 1:3–4)

9. You will learn to give thanks in everything. (1 Thessalonians 5:18)

10. You will remember that nothing can separate us from the love of Christ. (Romans 8:35–39)

order information

To order additional copies of this book, please visit
www.redemption-press.com.
Also available on Amazon.com and BarnesandNoble.com
or by calling toll-free 1-844-2REDEEM.

CPSIA information can be obtained
at www.ICGtesting.com
Printed in the USA
FSHW020613070620
70953FS

9 781646 450527